For Both Resting and Breeding

For Both Resting and Breeding

Adam Meisner

For Both Resting and Breeding
first published 2023 by Scirocco Drama
An imprint of J. Gordon Shillingford Publishing Inc.
© 2023 Adam Meisner

Scirocco Drama Editor: Glenda MacFarlane
Cover design by Doowah Design
Author photo by Mike Steinhauer
Production photos by Katie Edwards

Printed and bound in Canada on 100% post-consumer recycled paper.
We acknowledge the financial support of the Manitoba Arts Council and
The Canada Council for the Arts for our publishing program.

Production inquiries to:
adamwmeisner@gmail.com

Library and Archives Canada Cataloguing in Publication

Title: For both resting and breeding / Adam Meisner.
Names: Meisner, Adam, author.
Description: A play.
Identifiers: Canadiana 2022049259X | ISBN 9781990738203 (softcover)
Classification: LCC PS8626.E395 F67 2023 | DDC C812/.6—dc23

J. Gordon Shillingford Publishing
P.O. Box 86, RPO Corydon Avenue, Winnipeg, MB Canada R3M 3S3

For Adam Welch, the first reader of this play and its loving champion

Adam Meisner

Adam Meisner was born in Moncton, New Brunswick and now lives in Ottawa on the unceded, unsurrendered Territory of the Anishinaabe Algonquin Nation. Adam's play *For Both Resting and Breeding* premiered at Talk Is Free Theatre in Barrie, Ontario in 2018, and the company toured the play to the Adelaide Festival in Australia in 2020. Adam's other writing has appeared in literary journals across North America and in several anthologies. Adam studied theatre at the University of Toronto and the University of Manchester and holds an MFA in Creative Writing from the University of British Columbia.

Acknowledgements

Many friends and collaborators brought *For Both Resting and Breeding* to life. Brandon Crone, who directed the first two productions, has my profound thanks for the play's development, providing crucial dramaturgical support and conducting workshops with actors. Brandon's commitment made all the difference. Thanks to Arkady Spivak for his unwavering support and for producing this play at Talk Is Free Theatre with great care and imagination. I also want to thank Maja Ardal for her dramaturgical wisdom and for her foreword to this publication. Thanks to the team at Scirocco Drama for their work on this publication: Karen Haughian, Glenda MacFarlane, Ashley Nielsen, Cori Jones, Heidi Harms, and Doowah Design. For their financial support to workshop this play, I am grateful to the Ontario Arts Council.

I am indebted to many readers and performers of this play at its various stages whose crucial reflections and insights informed its development. I want to thank Lynn McGuigan for creating the Ottawa Little Theatre Playwrights' Circle, among the first readers of *For Both Resting and Breeding*. My thanks to the actors for the first staged reading of this play at the Safe Words Festival in 2016: Jakob Ehman, Thomas Gough, Marcia Johnson, Andrew Moodie, Rose Napoli, and Vanessa Smythe. Thanks to those actors who workshoped this play in 2017: Thomas Gough, Marcia Johnson, Jackie Rowland, Heath V. Salazar, and Adriano Sobretodo, Jr.

Thank you to all the actors, designers, and theatre professionals who brought this play to life in its first production in 2018: Maja Ardal, Beth Elliot, Jakob Ehman, Holly Lloyd, Xavier Lopez,

Milly Maguire, Joe Pagan, Vanessa Smythe, and Alexander Thomas. I am equally indebted to those who remounted it in 2020 for its tour to Australia: Maja Ardal, Jeff Braunstein, Laura Delchiaro, Amy Keating, Richard Lam, Milly Maguire, Jamie McRoberts, Joe Pagan, Ken James Stewart, and Alexander Thomas.

Finally, I want to thank my partner, Adam Welch, for his ongoing enthusiasm for this play. I am forever grateful to my parents, Timothy and Janice, for their ongoing encouragement of my writing, without which the world of the Ishes would not exist.

Playwright's Note

What do you remember about the year 2000? (If, like me, you were alive?)

Who were you in that year? How did you live? How did those around you live? Were you like the people around you, or was there something that marked you as different?

Was it a happy time or fraught? Or is it possible to remember the past in a more nuanced way, neither golden nor dark age?

Do you think any part of your life from that year will survive for future people to discover? Which parts will carry on? Which will be lost? And why?

These are some of the larger questions I grappled with as I wrote For Both Resting and Breeding, a play about people in the year 2150 trying to recreate millennial life. I chose the year 2000 as the play's focus for many reasons. For one, the year marks the start of a new century and a new millennium, so I suspect future historians will study it closely for that simple, if somewhat arbitrary, reason. The year seemed close enough for me to remember in vivid detail, but also afforded enough distance so that I could study it as a historian might.

More than this, I chose the year 2000 because I came of age that year. I was sixteen going on seventeen. I lived in Orléans, a suburb east of Ottawa, Canada's capital. I lived with my parents, my younger brother, and our Airedale Terrier in a four-bedroom, two-car garage house with a pool in the backyard. I worked part-time as a lifeguard and swimming instructor. I played basketball, wrote poetry, and acted in high school plays (I think we performed *Guys and Dolls* that year). In other words, I lived a relatively privileged, happy life.

But the year wasn't entirely carefree. I started to come out as gay to friends and family. This wasn't an easy thing to do at that time or place. My nearest and dearest were relatively accepting and supportive, and not entirely surprised by this: my parents had thought I was transgender as a child and took me to a psychologist to explore my gender identity, something that now seems to me progressive for the early 1990s. But I kept this truth hidden from many, afraid that people at school and work might shun me, and that a gay-bashing lurked around every corner. The shame and stigma of the AIDS crisis meant I was also afraid of contracting HIV and dying young—something I suspected was inevitable, largely on account of the small-minded and limited sex education offered by my Catholic high school.

For years, I tried unsuccessfully to write a play about gender and sexuality set against the backdrop of my millennial suburban youth. Frustrated by my attempts, I decided to try something new: I would write a play that was without gender and sexuality, a play that wasn't set in the year 2000. I thought this would be no more than an exercise, but it led me to the world of *For Both Resting and Breeding*—a play that, curiously, took me back to the very subject and setting the exercise meant to avoid.

At first, I thought I was creating a utopia with the world of this play. Without gender and sexuality, this world would have no homophobia, no transphobia, no misogyny, no rape, and no struggle for reproductive rights. How wonderful! But it soon occurred to me that this world would also lack many positive aspects of gender and sexuality, like the joys of sex. I also started to think of the other positive things from the year 2000 that this future world might lack, and a more complex future emerged.

I did not write this play with a singular argument, position, or warning about gender, sexuality, or anything else in mind. I allowed myself to work with a sense of curiosity. I believe artists and audiences are at their best when they remain curious and ask questions rather than dictate positions. That said, at the time of writing this note, politicians around the world continue to make decisions that negatively affect, and sometimes even threaten, the lives of queer and trans people (and especially youth). And so, in that context, I want to emphasize that this play believes a future with a diversity of genders and sexual expressions is desirable to one without, and we would be wise to advocate for that future.

Of course, *For Both Resting and Breeding* touches on more than gender and sexuality. It also considers the possible histories of work, food, the arts, sleep, housing, communities, cities, fashion, the environment, and technology—and more. Some of these explorations are more oblique than others, encouraging artists and audiences to use their imaginations to fill in the blanks about what has happened between the years 2000 and 2150. I hope this adds to the fun.

As I worked on this play, I became more interested in its preoccupations with collective memory than with gender and sexuality. I wrote the first iteration of this play as Canada approached its sesquicentennial. At that time, I was thinking a lot about how the country commemorated its past, and how it wilfully forgot so much else. I recalled the heritage-house museums I visited, and adored, as a child; as an adult, I realized they had elided so much of their colonial past.

If nothing else, I hope this play inspires audiences to think about collective memory. Who decides what gets remembered? How do people remember together? And to what end? For me, these questions seem essential to understanding our past as fully as possible and, in turn, creating a better future for everyone, with all our brilliant differences.

Adam Meisner
October 2022

Foreword

There are few playwrights daring enough to imagine our future—Adam Meisner is one of them. He has created a world with *For Both Resting and Breeding*, and he delivers a unique theatrical vision for audiences to marvel and ponder.

I was a cast member with the inaugural production for Talk Is Free Theatre in Barrie, Ontario, and I also performed in the touring production to the Adelaide Festival, Australia, in early 2020. In both productions, I played ISH62, a historian who sees the past as "something to which we should never return."

As an actor it was a terrific challenge to perform a character who is part of a genderless society that has seemingly forgotten social and sexual intimacy, rancour, and passion in favour of peace. Adam's play invites actors and audience to look back at life at the turn of the twenty-first century, and to interpret it from the perspective of the Ishes—nameless, genderless characters identified only by their age.

The Ishes believe that they live more serene lives than their ancestors. They live alone in "personal spaces" (they value their alone time). They come together purely for shared tasks, not out of any emotional impulse. And when they speak to one another their sentences are often short and telegraphic. They might sound curt to our contemporary ears, but their use of language stems from a desire to be efficient and avoid confusion that could lead to conflict.

Adam has crafted a play with a perfect balance of humour and melancholy. At times the play seems to be a drama, at others a comedy. (At some performances it landed more strongly on one side than the other, as if the audience on a particular night had made an unspoken decision about the kind of play they were seeing.)

The actors in both productions were thoroughly engaged in creating a collective understanding of this future community and the history that led to its creation. We enthusiastically participated in building our new world and inventing ourselves as Ishes.

The opportunity to look at family life in 2000 through the eyes of the Ish historians brings the characters into a dilemma of temptation. What was it really like to live as a millennial suburban family? Adam cleverly has the Ish community unravel into a state of near-chaos as they bumble through their attempt to understand and represent the lives of millennial people.

This future world is probable, possible, and rather peculiar to us, but it leaves us wondering if this may be a genuine outcome of our current moment. After all, our present world is unsustainable as it struggles with its prejudices and discrimination, poverty, over-population, wars, and a climate catastrophe.

Maja Ardal
Actor and Playwright

Production History

For Both Resting and Breeding first received a staged reading at the Safe Words Festival in Toronto, Ontario on June 17, 2016. Safe Words subsequently workshopped the play with a grant from the Ontario Arts Council.

Talk Is Free Theatre produced the first production of *For Both Resting and Breeding*, April 12–21, 2018, in Barrie, Ontario.

Talk Is Free Theatre subsequently toured the play to the Adelaide Festival in Australia, February 18–March 3, 2020.

The following cast and creative team were involved in the Talk Is Free productions:

2020 Cast

Maja Ardal	ISH62
Amy Keating	ISH34
Richard Lam	ISH40
Jamie McRoberts	ISH20
Alexander Thomas	ISH84

2018 Cast

Maja Ardal	ISH62
Jakob Ehman	ISH40
Xavier Lopez	ISH34
Vanessa Smythe	ISH20
Alexander Thomas	ISH84

Creative team

Brandon Crone...Director (2018, 2020)

Laura Delchiaro.......................................Costume Designer (2020)

Holly Lloyd ....Costume and Props Designer (2018)

Milly Maguire.................................... Stage Manager (2018, 2020)

Jeff Braunstein...Stage Manager (2020)

Joe Pagan .... Set and Lighting Design (2018, 2020)

Ken James Stewart....................Apprentice Stage Manager (2020)

Beth Elliot.... Production Manager and Technical Director (2018)

The Ishes inspect artifacts in the millennial house that they will convert into a museum. From left: ISH34 (Amy Keating), ISH84 (Alexander Thomas), ISH20 (Jamie McRoberts), and ISH40 (Richard Lam). Photograph by: Katie Edwards.

ISH84 (Alexander Thomas) reads a millennial-era romance novel discovered among the artifacts for their museum by ISH34 (Amy Keating). Photograph by: Katie Edwards.

The Ishes explore a trove of millennial-era objects found in the Big Dig of 2148, including paper clips, wires, sunglasses, cellphones, and other mysterious relics. From left: ISH34 (Amy Keating), ISH62 (Maja Ardal), ISH40 (Richard Lam), and ISH20 (Jamie McRoberts). Photograph by: Katie Edwards.

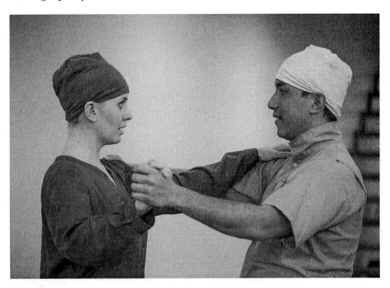

ISH20 (Jamie McRoberts) and ISH40 (Richard Lam) dance as millennials – but at a safe distance. Photograph by: Katie Edwards.

ISH40 (Richard Lam) and ISH20 (Jamie McRoberts) sit on the sofa and pretend to watch TV as a millennial husband and wife. Photograph by: Katie Edwards.

ISH84 (Alexander Thomas), dressed up as a millennial grandmother, demonstrates how to make a millennial treat: chocolate chip cookies. Photograph by: Katie Edwards.

ISH20 (Jamie McRoberts) begs ISH62 (Maja Ardal) to wear a Jennifer Aniston-style millennial dress in their museum while ISH34 (Amy Keating), dressed as a teenaged boy, watches uncomfortably. Photograph by: Katie Edwards.

ISH20 enters the museum dressed as a pregnant millennial woman to the shock of ISH62 (Maja Ardal) and ISH40 (Richard Lam). Photograph by: Katie Edwards.

Characters

The characters live in a gender-neutral world: they dress the same, style their hair mostly the same, and use similar mannerisms and vocal intonations (and where these differ from person to person, they are not easily marked as masculine or feminine).

The numbers in each character's name refers to the character's age, while the "ish" in front of the number is a gender-neutral pronoun simultaneously replacing she/her/hers and he/him/his in the world of the play. The "ish" pronoun is different from the gender non-binary they/them/theirs, as the world of the ishes is without a binary and all people use ish.

ISH62 — a historian

ISH40 — a historian and ISH62's colleague

ISH34 — a structural engineer

ISH20 — a university student

ISH84 — an elder

Setting

The main floor of a suburban family house built in 1999, now many years into the future (2150). The house is decrepit—doors hanging off hinges, boarded-up windows, spindles missing from the staircase, etc.—but the state seems to reflect neglect and the passage of time rather than violence. In fact, the house might seem as though it was never lived in—the walls still builder's white, some of the windows never opened.

ACT ONE

Scene 1

A late-November light.

The main floor of a decrepit house: open concept with the front hall leading into living room, dining room, and kitchen. Poor lighting so that it looks as though the house might be somewhere underground — but enough light to see.

ISH62 enters, looks around the house, decides that it is ugly.

ISH40 enters behind, enthusiastic.

ISH62:   This?

ISH40:   The house.

ISH62:   No.

ISH62 turns to leave but ISH40 stands in the way.

ISH40:   Wait.

ISH62:   No.

ISH40:   Look.

ISH62:   Have looked.

ISH40:   Keep looking.

                *ISH40 takes ISH62's hand to lead ish back
                into the house.*

ISH62:   Let-go-let-go-let-go—

ISH40:   I want you to see!

ISH62:   I saw!

ISH40:   I want you to see what I see.

ISH62:   Never see what you see.

                *ISH62 turns to leave and ISH40 stands in
                the way once more.*

ISH40:   Listen—

ISH62:   Cannot.

ISH40:   All their dreams and aspirations.

ISH62:   Where?

ISH40:   *(Walking around the space.)* Open-concept.
                (Motioning to the kitchen.) Granite countertops.
                (Walking back.) Hardwood. Dark hardwood.
                Coffee-coloured. What they wanted. Matching
                cabinets too. *(Pointing around to various
                aspects of the house.)* Matching, matching,
                matching, complementary, matching. *This*
                was beautiful.

ISH62:   Was beautiful.

ISH40:   Point of the house is the was.

ISH62:   Ceiling is—

                *ISH62 points to a small brown spot on the
                ceiling.*

ISH40:   An old leak.

ISH62:   Could be dangerous.

ISH40:   Will get an engineer.

ISH62:   And if the engineer says structurally unsound?

ISH40:   Then, of course, no. But if ish says is fine, then yes.

ISH62:   And who will do the rest of the work?

ISH40:   Volunteers.

ISH62:   Would never find enough volunteers.

ISH40:   For a project like this, we will find a world of volunteers.

ISH62 looks around skeptically.

ISH62:   How long do we have?

ISH40:   For the city's sesquicentennial.

ISH62:   A month, then.

ISH40:   Five weeks.

ISH62:   Impossible.

ISH40:   No, it *is* possible.

ISH62:   To create an entire past world?

ISH40:   No, to re-create a small part of the past.

ISH62:   A lot of work to get it right.

ISH40:   You always wanted to do something like this. Always said you thought it would help people remember the past. Dream of a lifetime.

ISH62:   Place smells like wet dog. And pistachios.

ISH40:	What do *pistachios* smell like?
ISH62:	Like this.

ISH62 about to leave, and then —

ISH40:	This is the last house built in 1999 that is still standing in our city. When the city was a suburb. A Mimosa Development. This model: The Oakwood.
ISH62:	*(Suddenly intrigued.)* Information about the tenants?
ISH40:	None.
ISH62:	Lost in the Erasure?
ISH40:	Exactly. Ours to interpret according to imagination.
ISH62:	Do not trust imagination.
ISH40:	Then ours to interpret according to the best available historical record.
ISH62:	Sounds better.
ISH40:	How do you want people to remember the past?
ISH62:	Something to which we should never return.
ISH40:	There is enough time for us to do that.

ISH62 walks around the space hesitantly while ISH40 admires the details of the house.

ISH62:	Safety first.
ISH40:	Safety always first.
ISH62:	Always. And then authenticity.

ISH40:	Yes, and then authenticity. Everything in keeping with the historical record.

A pause.

ISH62:	Fine.
ISH40:	Yes?
ISH62:	Yes.
ISH40:	To see the upstairs?
ISH62:	Not necessary. If we do this, only display the main floor. Not interested in explaining bedroom history.
ISH40:	Only five weeks to do this, anyway.
ISH62:	Exactly!

ISH40 goes to hug ISH62.

ISH62:	Work to do before celebrating.
ISH40:	Where to begin?
ISH62:	You get the volunteers, I will start with a schedule.
ISH40:	Yes!
ISH62:	Work to do!

ISH62 exits.

ISH40 skips around the house with excitement mounting and then runs out after ISH62.

Scene 2

A brighter day with light in the house for the first time in many decades.

Some cleaning has taken place. The walls appear whiter, the floors swept, debris cleared away.

ISH34 — an engineer — wanders around the space, inspecting the house: ceiling, staircase leading to the second floor, windows, etc.

ISH20 and ISH84 — volunteers — stand awkwardly at the centre, looking around the house and waiting.

ISH40 stands by the door waiting for ISH62 to join them. A nervous pause, then:

ISH40:   Just a minute more!

ISH20 and ISH84 nod, then begin a conversation with one another:

ISH84:   Is fascinating.

ISH20:   Yes.

ISH84:   Needs work, though.

ISH20:   Yes.

ISH84:   Easy enough.

ISH20:   Yes.

ISH84:   Why we are here.

ISH20:   Yes.

ISH62 rushes into the room.

ISH62:	I-am-here-I-am-here—hello-I-am—here. *(Looks around the house.)* Looks better. Smells lemony! *(Notices the two volunteers, turns to ISH40 quietly.)* Only three volunteers?
ISH40:	Two. *(Pointing to ISH34.)* Ish is an engineer.
ISH62:	Only two?
ISH40:	But we can use the engineer for more than just inspecting.
ISH62:	You promised a world of volunteers.
ISH40:	And this is the world we have to work with. *(Points to ISH20.)* Ish was my student last term, *(Points to ISH84.)* and ish found my call for volunteers on a community board.
ISH62:	Make do if we must.
ISH40:	More than make do. Will excel!
ISH62:	*(To ISH34.)* Verdict on the structure?
ISH34:	Stable. I think.
ISH62:	Just think?
ISH34:	Pretty sure.
ISH62:	And the ceiling?
ISH34:	Minor leak. If anything, more worried about the walls. *(Goes over to a wall and listens closely.)* Rodents ruin heritage.
ISH40:	Now, how should we do this?
ISH62:	Let us form a circle at the centre of the room.
ISH20:	And sit?
ISH62:	Sure. *(To ISH34.)* You too.

ISH34:   Am the engineer.

ISH62:   Oh no, no, no. You are much more than that.

ISH34:   Much more than an—?

> *ISH62 brings ISH34 to join the group.*

ISH62:   Yes. Everybody sit down.

> *They all consider the floor, but it is still extremely dirty. ISH20 sits quickly. ISH84 tries to sit, but quickly gets up.*

ISH84:   Can we stand?

ISH34:   Sweeped already.

ISH62:   Swept. You mean swept.

ISH40:   Stand and sit, as you like.

ISH20:   The floor is damp.

ISH62:   Everybody standing then! Are we in a circle?

> *They shift around to make a perfect circle, ISH62 adjusting their positions minutely.*

ISH40:   Is this perfection necessary?

ISH62:   Yes.

> *The perfect circle is formed.*

ISH40:   Shall we begin?

ISH62:   Proceed.

ISH40:   Let us go around the circle and say why we are here.

ISH62:   Do not overthink.

ISH40:   State the first reason that comes to mind.

ISH62:   We can go around the circle as many times as we like.

ISH40:   And we will use this womp. *(ISH40 retrieves a glowing ball from ish pocket.)* When the previous speaker tosses it to you, it is your turn to say something. Let me begin: To celebrate the anniversary of M City.

ISH62:   There is the obvious.

ISH40:   No wrong reasons. Your turn.

ISH40 passes the womp to ISH62.

ISH62:   To show the past as it was.

ISH40:   Also obvious.

ISH62:   No wrong reasons.

ISH62 tosses it to ISH34.

ISH34:   Uh. To be your engineer.

ISH62:   Sure. Anything more?

ISH34:   Uhhhh—

ISH84 takes the womp from ISH34.

ISH84:   What about to meet new people?

ISH40:   Yes. Good.

ISH84 tosses the womp to ISH20.

ISH20:   To help others remember the past?

ISH62:   Yes, that is an important one. Dangerous to forget the past. Keep going.

ISH20 hands the womp back to ISH34.

ISH34:   How about . . . to know?

A brief pause.

ISH62:   Know what?

ISH34:   The past?

ISH62:   Yes, okay, fine. But—

ISH40:   No wrong reasons, keep going.

    ISH34 quickly tosses the womp to ISH84.

ISH84:   How about to appreciate what we have?

ISH62:   Yes! A very good one!

ISH20:   Oh!

    ISH20 grabs the womp from ISH84.

ISH20:   And to appreciate what we do not have.

ISH62:   Well—

ISH40:   No wrong reasons! Keep going!

    ISH20 hands the womp back to ISH34.

ISH34:   Uhhhhh–do not know.

ISH40:   Anything!

ISH34:   Uh. To try.

ISH62:   Try what?

ISH34:   To try what the past…feels like?

ISH62:   What in particular?

ISH34:   Uh. Do not know.

    ISH84 takes the womp from ISH34.

ISH84:   Maybe to try what the clothes felt like?

ISH40:   Yes! Next!

ISH84 tosses the womp to ISH20.

ISH20:   To find inspiration in the past.

ISH62:   Inspiration—there is an old-fashioned word!

ISH40:   Keep going.

ISH20 tosses the womp to ISH34.

ISH34:   To remember.

ISH62:   Let us go deeper. To remember what, exactly?

ISH34:   Am not very good at this.

ISH40:   Anything!

ISH84 takes the womp from ISH34.

ISH84:   To remember our ancestors.

ISH62:   Great.

ISH20:   Which ancestors?

ISH62:   Good questions. Let us be specific. Surely we do not want to remember all of our ancestors.

A collective laugh.

ISH84:   Want to remember my great-gran Jennifer. Have Jennifer's email log. Survived the erasure. A printout. Have read it many times and always wondered what it was like for ish. *She.* Do not know what to call Jennifer.

ISH62:   *She* is fine. What else about Jennifer?

ISH84:   Jennifer liked to show off, always sending body photos to boyfriends.

ISH40:   Maybe you could bring in that email log to share with us someday as part of our preparatory research.

ISH62:   Just the log, no need for the photos.

ISH40:   Keep going.

           ISH34 takes the womp from ISH84.

ISH34:   What about to restore this house to its former
           glory?

ISH40:   Yes, yes, yes!

ISH62:   In part.

ISH40:   No judgment.

ISH62:   Glory is a word that invites judgment.

ISH34:   Meaning?

ISH62:   Meaning you are making a judgment that the
           house was once glorious.

ISH34:   Meant better than this.

ISH62:   Define better.

ISH34:   Meant as it was. Restore its structural integ-
           rity. That would be better.

ISH62:   Yes, fine. That is all I wanted to—

           *IHS34 tosses the womp to ISH20, who
           holds it for a hesitant moment before—*

ISH20:   What about to be a woman?

           *This answer surprises the group, and
           everybody is quiet for a moment as they
           contemplate this.*

ISH62:   *(Nervous.)* Explain?

ISH20:   Want to do this because I have always wanted
           to know what it was like to be a woman.

ISH62:   Well...

ISH40:   No judgment.

ISH62:   No, but—

ISH20:   What?

ISH40:   Part of this experiment will involve dressing up like millennials, and we will have to perform the parts of men and women from that period.

ISH20:   When I was a child, I always wondered what it would have been like to be a girl. This might sound peculiar, but . . . always felt like I would have liked to be a girl.

The most uncomfortable kind of silence.

ISH62:   Uh—

ISH20:   Like it would have been natural for me to be a—

ISH62:   Yes, but it was not. Natural. To be a boy or a girl or anything else for that matter.

ISH20:   No, I know that.

ISH62:   Must be careful.

ISH40:   Say it without the word *natural*. Try *comfortable* instead.

ISH62:   It was not comfortable!

ISH40:   Ish is only saying that ish would like to try what it was like to be a girl or a woman.

ISH62 takes the womp from ISH20.

ISH62:   Fine. That is fine. We will try that. But—

ISH40:   Let us not get overwhelmed. Is only the beginning.

ISH62:   Do not want us to fantasize about what it meant to be a boy or a girl or a man or a woman. There was nothing wonderful about being trapped in those roles.

ISH20:   Am sorry. Did not mean to imply that it would have been wonderful to be a girl or woman.

ISH62:   Am only clarifying the historicist position we are taking here. Must represent the past objectively.

ISH20:   Is it objective to say that men and women were trapped?

ISH62:   We have recorded accounts to explain that they were *trapped*. You know the history—we all do.

ISH84:   Yes, we all do. Or we should.

ISH20:   Right.

ISH40:   In any event, there is nothing wrong with wanting to try on the past—the lives of both men and women. That is how we will help those who are less familiar with the past to remember. And all of us will have different parts of the project that interest us the most. For my part, I have always wondered what it would be like to live in a family unit. Several people together in such a big building! Sometimes at odds with one another, sometimes in perfect harmony. Imagine what that would have been like. And that is what we are going to recreate right here, in this house: a nuclear, millennial family unit—men and women and—and—

ISH34:   Will we have children?

ISH62:   Clearly there are no children here, so no.

ISH40:   Perhaps we will make believe our family has children, but they will not be present at the museum.

ISH20:   Maybe the family has teenaged children?

ISH34:   Who will play the mom and dad?

ISH62:   We are not deciding that today. And would like us to try on all the parts so that each of us gets a rounded view of the past—

ISH40:   Which is not to say we cannot have fun doing it.

ISH62:   Did not say that.

ISH40:   Only clarifying.

ISH84:   Wait. Clarifying what?

ISH34:   Confused now.

ISH62:   See, now you have confused everybody.

ISH20:   *(To ISH62.)* Think it is the bit you were saying that got us confused.

ISH62:   What bit?

ISH34:   Are we still giving our reasons for being here?

ISH40 takes the womp from ISH62 and puts it away.

ISH40:   Think we should stop before we get any more confused.

ISH62:   Fine. I have schedules for all of you. *(ISH62 hands out a toothpick-like object—some sort of technology that they recognize.)* Go back tonight and read. The next few weeks: decorating, assembling furniture, making costumes, finding props, studying the lives of the millennials so that we are ready to show an accurate picture of the past to the people of M City on anniversary day.

ISH40:   Questions?

ISH84:   Not for me.

ISH20:   Or me.

ISH34:   Uh. Or me.

ISH62:   Perfect clarity, then?

A pause.

ISH40:   If only. Thank you for coming.

ISH20 and ISH84:   Thank you.

ISH20:   Am sorry if I—

ISH40:   Do not be sorry. We are all learning.

ISH20 and ISH84 exit, but ISH62 stops ISH34 before leaving.

ISH62:   Hope you do not mind helping us with other things, aside from the structural review.

ISH40:   Painting and such.

ISH62:   And maybe a little recreation, too?

ISH34:   Do not know.

ISH62:   A team project. Promise it will be fun—we need you!

ISH34 exits quickly.

ISH40:   Think that went well.

ISH62:   Did it?

ISH40:   Think this is going to be interesting.

ISH62:   The word *interesting* is without meaning.

ISH40:   Think this is going to be powerful then.

ISH62:   Let us not scare them away.

ISH40:   Agreed. There is nothing wrong with trying things on.

ISH62:   If it is only trying them on. Would not want to revive old ideas.

ISH40:   No, of course not.

ISH62:   *(In an old upper-class Manhattan drawl.)* "It's very difficult to keep the line between the past and the present."

ISH40:   What is that?

ISH62:   A line from a movie. A very old movie. A documentary.

ISH40:   You watch movies?

ISH62:   My first major research project was on the last days of professional movies. Do you watch movies?

ISH40:   Sometimes.

ISH62:   The people who lived here probably liked to watch movies.

ISH40:   They had no idea what was coming for them.

ISH62:   The Advent of the Great Busy-ness City.

ISH40:   Followed quickly by the End of Work.

ISH62:   The Long Thaw.

ISH40:   And the Great Transition.

ISH62:   Everything about to be transformed.

ISH40:   Not right away, though.

ISH62:   Only coming.

ISH40:   Soon.

> *Blackout.*

Scene 3

> *Suddenly sunshine in the house.*
>
> *ISH34 busily inspects various parts of the room: the banister, a wall, the floorboards, etc.*
>
> *ISH40 enters with a stack of paint swatches in hand, which ish lays out on the floor in front of ISH20.*

ISH20:   What are these?

ISH40:   Called paint swatches. People used to look at them to pick out paint colours.

ISH20:   So many options.

ISH40:   Millennials liked to have many options.

ISH20:   But they are all red.

ISH40:   To you and me, yes—but for millennials, many kinds of red. Have canisters of paint for each of these shades of red in the archive. Thought we could choose a shade and then paint one of the walls by the entrance to the museum.

ISH20:   Only one wall?

ISH40:   Something they did. Called it an accent wall.

ISH20:   What were they accenting?

ISH40:   The wall.

ISH20:   The answers are always obvious.

ISH40:   Which colour do you like the most?

ISH20:   (Selecting a colour swatch.) Maybe…this one?

ISH40:   Ah, yes. Guess what they called this red?

                A curious pause.

ISH20:   Bright red?

ISH40:   Imagination!

ISH20:   Did they have imaginations back then?

ISH40:   To sell things.

ISH20:   Ha!

ISH40:   Guess the name of the colour!

                A flustered pause.

ISH20:   Do not know. Ruby?

ISH40:   No. More playful.

ISH20:   Candy ruby?

ISH40:   Close! Candy apple.

ISH20:   Quaint.

>   *ISH20 holds the chosen paint swatch up and studies it closely, trying to image an entire wall in this colour, while ISH40 gathers up the other paint swatches.*
>
>   *ISH34 exits the house to get something and ISH20 turns anxiously towards ISH40.*

ISH20:   What I said at the first meeting about thinking it would be natural for me to be...

ISH40:   Yes?

ISH20:   Did not mean that.

ISH40:   No?

ISH20:   Do not know.

ISH40:   It is safe to mean whatever you want to mean with me.

ISH20:   Is it?

ISH40:   Want it to be.

ISH20:   Suppose I meant...always wondered what it would be like to make myself as pretty as possible, to stand out—and to be admired for that prettiness. To be beautiful, really. Like a millennial woman. *(A pause.)* Should not have said that aloud. Full of funny ideas about the past.

ISH40:   Is fine with me! *(An idea occurs to ish.)* Oh! I have something you might like.

>   *ISH40 puts down the paint swatches, turns to a nearby box, and retrieves a pair of high-heel shoes.*

ISH20:   Are these—real?

ISH40:   Yes! Try them on? Do not fit me.

ISH20 takes the shoes with hesitation, admires them for a moment, and then puts them on.

ISH40:   Try walking!

ISH20 clomps around in the shoes.

ISH20:   Very elegant!

ISH20's clomping turns to skipping, dancing, and, finally, elation!

ISH40:   You like them?

ISH20:   Love them! Feel so pretty!

ISH20 skips over to ISH40 and—almost by accident—kisses ish on the cheek, then takes a surprised step back.

ISH20:   I—

ISH40:   That—

ISH20:   Did not mean—

ISH40:   We should—

ISH20:   Sorry.

ISH20 takes off the shoes and hands them to ISH40 who puts them back in a box somewhere hidden in the house. ISH40 gathers up the paint swatches once more, and ISH20 holds out the candy apple paint swatch to inspect it again.

ISH20:   This colour looks…

ISH40:   Strange?

ISH20:   To me.

ISH40:   To me, too. But the past often looks strange.

> *ISH34 returns with some sort of curious-looking tool and looks at the chosen paint swatch with ISH20 and ISH40.*

ISH34:   Huh.

ISH40:   What does this colour look like to you?

ISH34:   Violent.

ISH40:   Think they would have thought dynamic.

ISH20:   Risky?

ISH34:   Daring?

ISH40:   What about funky?

ISH20 and ISH34: Funky!

ISH40:   Maybe funky was outmoded by 2000.

ISH20:   Like it all the same.

> *ISH34 proceeds to apply the tool to some task in the room.*

> *ISH40 looks around at the rest of the house. It suddenly pales against the accent wall.*

ISH40:   Maybe they were accenting how boring everything was around them.

ISH20:   Think the past was probably very interesting—much more interesting than life now.

ISH40:   One's own time is never very interesting, is it?

ISH20:   According to you, the historian!

ISH40:   Ha! A good point!

                *ISH34 notices a shift in ISH20 and ISH40's
                dynamic and becomes intrigued by them at
                a remove.*

ISH20:   Thank you.

ISH40:   Shall we go paint the entrance wall now?

ISH20:   Yes!

ISH40:   Will do it with rolling brushes.

ISH20:   Brushes to *roll* the paint?

ISH40:   Follow me—will show you!

ISH20:   Am learning so much already!

                *ISH40 and ISH20 exit, a tangible energy of
                excitement growing between them.*

                *ISH34 studies them as they leave, then
                follows closely behind.*

Scene 4

                *A new day. Now a table and chairs in the
                dining room at which ISH84 and ISH34 sit
                among piles of old books, each one reading
                something.*

                *In the background, ISH40 and ISH20
                at opposite sides of the room, tending to
                various tasks (tidying, cleaning spots on
                the floor, etc.). They look at one another
                surreptitiously with interest and longing.*

                *After a moment of reading, ISH34 closes
                the book ish was reading and pushes it
                aside.*

ISH84:	Finished your book already?
ISH34:	No. Had enough. Do not like it.
ISH84:	Why not?
ISH34:	Pointless.
ISH84:	Maybe for us, but books were not pointless for the millennials.
ISH34:	Do not understand the point even for them.
ISH84:	Many reasons for them.
ISH34:	Such as?
ISH84:	Sometimes for information. Sometimes for pleasure. Sometimes both.
ISH34:	This one all pleasure, no information.
ISH84:	Is that a terrible thing?
ISH34:	Prefer information.
ISH84:	Let me see what you chose.

ISH34 hands ISH84 a romance novel.

ISH34:	About a man and a woman on a ranch. But no cattle. Want to learn more about cattle, but where are the cattle?
ISH84:	This is a cheap romance. How did that get in our pile?
ISH34:	Do not know.
ISH84:	None of us would like that. Try this one instead.

ISH84 retrieves a new book from the pile and tucks the other one away.

ISH34:   What?

ISH84:   Something my great-gran liked as a child.

ISH34:   About?

ISH84:   Wizards. Magic spells. Good. Evil.

ISH34:   The point is pleasure, then?

ISH84:   In a way. Also to teach children lessons.

ISH34:   About?

ISH84:   Do not know, actually. Read it to find out!

ISH34:   Right. To report back?

ISH84:   No. Just for yourself. For your own pleasure perhaps.

ISH34:   Not sure.

ISH84:   Or think of it as a story that will give you information.

ISH34:   But is made up.

ISH84:   Yes, of course. But was made up to mirror the millennial world. You understand?

ISH34:   Right.

ISH62 barges into the room.

ISH62:   Quiz time!

ISH20:   Quiz time?

ISH62:   As in the olden millennial days! Loved to test. Quiz. Stump. Ready?

They gather round.

ISH40:   Ready!

ISH62:   You start?

ISH40:   Uh. Fine. Uh. An easy question?

ISH62:   Easy to start, trouble it as we go!

ISH40:   Sure. Founding year of the Ultimate Connector.

ISH34:   1992!

ISH62:   Correct. And good question. Everyone knew that?

ISH20:   I think so.

ISH62:   Does not seem like all of you knew that.

ISH34:   Of course.

ISH62:   Need to be sure we know all the capstones. Next one?

ISH40:   Your turn.

ISH62:   A little more difficult?

ISH34:   Yes!

ISH62:   Peak year of the 20th century Plague?

ISH20:   Do not know that one.

ISH62:   Try!

ISH34:   1997?

ISH40:   Close, actually.

ISH20:   Are there any culture-related questions?

ISH62:   We are not done with this question—

ISH34:   1995?

ISH62:   Correct!

ISH34:   Guessed the answer.

ISH20:   Please, just one cultural question?

ISH62:   All of this is cultural, history is cultural.

ISH20:   This sounds scientific. I mean something like, who sang the hit single from the year 2000 "Independent Women Part 1?"

ISH34:   Was there a Part 2?

ISH62:   Should be focusing on other things.

ISH84:   Beyoncé!

ISH62:   Who?

ISH20:   Almost! Give up?

ISH62:   Should be focusing on things like who were the final three Presidents of—

ISH20:   Destiny's Child. Regular mistake.

ISH62:   I do not think this information is relevant to—

ISH20:   Might have been relevant to millennials.

ISH62:   Maybe some of them. A small faction—a small, privileged faction of them. And an even tinier faction within that faction. Teenage girls, maybe.

ISH20:   What is wrong with learning about what was important to teenage girls?

ISH62:   Want us to know the bigger capstones first and foremost.

ISH20:   Maybe we should learn according to the parts we are going to play in the house.

ISH62:   Want us to play all the parts.

ISH84:   My memory cannot hold all that information.

ISH34:   Would be easier if you assigned us parts, and we could learn the information that would have been important to those parts.

ISH20:   Agreed.

ISH62:   Not sure I—

ISH40:   Well, why not?

A disgruntled pause.

ISH62:   Fine. If they must have parts, let us assign them parts.

ISH40:   One part for each of you. To make our millennial family.

ISH62:   Did we agree to make a family?

ISH40:   This is a house for a family so—

ISH20:   I want to play the teenage daughter.

ISH62:   That is not what I—

ISH34:   Could play the teenage son.

ISH62:   We were going to assign—

ISH84:   Always wanted to be a grandma!

ISH20:   *(To ISH40.)* That leaves you as our dad—

ISH62:   This is not a fantasy play game.

ISH20:   *(To ISH62.)* And you as our mom!

ISH62:   Mother. But really, I am not, uh, I would not make a very good—I am nothing like one of those.

ISH20:   No, none of us are anything like our parts. This is a play.

ISH62:   No, it is history.

ISH20:   Yes, but like a history play. And you are the director!

ISH62:   Am I?

ISH34:   Can we go back to the quiz, now?

ISH62:   Thought you found it too general.

ISH20:   General but fun!

ISH34:   Next question!

ISH20:   Make it a good one.

ISH84:   Yes, challenge us!

ISH62 is at a loss for a moment, then thinks up a question:

ISH62:   All right. In what year did the Great Transition begin?

Everyone is stumped.

ISH20:   Was there a beginning?

There is no answer.

Sunset to darkness.

Scene 5

> *Late night rain.*
>
> *ISH84 stands over the dining room table, flipping through old Hollywood tabloids.*
>
> *ISH62 carries a bin of fabric to the table.*

ISH84:   A lot of denim.

ISH62:   They wore a lot of denim.

> *More flipping through the magazine.*

ISH84:   *(Pointing to an image.)* Would prefer this.

ISH62:   Jennifer.

ISH84:   My great-grandmother's name.

ISH62:   Aniston.

ISH84:   A good model.

ISH62:   An actress.

ISH84:   Meant Jennifer Aniston is a good model of millennial life.

ISH62:   No. Not a real person. Aspirational.

ISH84:   Millennials were aspirational.

ISH62:   Not in a suburban house. People here would have been happy with their ordinary lives. *(ISH62 lays out some dark fabrics on the table.)* What about this for tops, and this for bottoms?

ISH84:   *(Looking back at the image of Jennifer Aniston.)* What about something more colorful—like this?

ISH62:   Called that lilac. Too pretty.

ISH84:   What is wrong with pretty?

ISH62:   Pretty is hypnotic.

ISH84:   Maybe some things in the past were hypnotic.

ISH62:   Only women would have worn that colour.

ISH84:   Yes. Dress would be for a woman.

ISH62:   Do not want to divide our house in two.

ISH84:   But they did.

ISH62:   Not sure. Still think denim bottoms and plain tops for all would be best.

ISH84:   They were not us.

ISH62:   They could have been.

                ISH84 hands over a magazine to ISH62 who flips through it quickly and then stops on a page.

ISH84:   What?

ISH62:   Aniston again. That woman was everywhere.

ISH84:   Movie premieres.

ISH62:   And advertisements for—water?

                ISH84 points to an image in the magazine.

ISH84:   Let me make this dress?

ISH62:   We are making the everyday here—and this is…very fashionable.

ISH84:   Even museums of the everyday can have special features. This could be our showstopper. *(ISH84 holds up a pastel-coloured fabric.)* Could make it in this? Am very skilled with fashion—but only ever make the same thing over and over again. Would like a challenge for once in my life.

The rain becomes heavier, and they both look up at the ceiling with concern.

ISH62:   Hope no leaks!

ISH84:   Would have been snow this time of year in my childhood.

ISH62:   You lived snow?

ISH84:   You did not?

ISH62:   In my birth year. But only that year. Do not remember it, but have seen images.

They listen to the rain.

ISH84:   Imagine if we could make snow for our museum.

ISH62:   Would be impossible. Need to focus on what is possible.

ISH84:   Like my showstopper dress?

A tense pause.

ISH62:   Oh, I do not know. Worried it might reinstate the ideals of womanly beauty.

ISH84 starts to stroke the pastel-coloured fabric.

ISH84:   My mother had a dress in this colour.

ISH62:   You had a mother.

ISH84:	Yes, of course. Forget we are not the same age.
ISH62:	Just that much younger. What was she like?
ISH84:	Lovely. But very difficult to talk about her.

ISH62 softens.

ISH62:	Fine. Make the dress.
ISH84:	Thank you.
ISH62:	But do not let it be too sexy!
ISH84:	Would never.

The light dims on ISH62's nervous energy.

Scene 6

A cold sunlight.

The ishes stand in a semi-circle around a mound of millennial objects.

ISH62:   And this is only skimming the surface of what we found in the Big Dig of 2148.

They begin exploring the objects.

ISH20:	So many paper clips.
ISH34:	*(Holding up a stapler.)* This?
ISH62:	Stapler. Do not press down.
ISH34:	Too rusted to press down.
ISH62:	Do not try.

ISH40 picks up a pair of sunglasses, puts them on.

ISH40:   Hey! Look! Sunglasses!

                  ISH40 looks funny to them, everyone laughs. ISH40 does a little dance and ISH20 laughs harder than everyone else.

ISH20:   *(Collapsing with laughter.)* Oh-oh-oh-oh!

ISH40:   I'm a coooooool dude.

ISH62:   What else?

ISH20:   *(Still laughing.)* Stop-stop-stop-or I am going to—

ISH40:   Stop or you will—what?

ISH62:   The sunglasses are not the correct period for our house.

ISH40:   No?

                  ISH62 takes the sunglasses off ISH40.

ISH62:   No. Those are from the 1980s, not the late nineties or early 2000s.

ISH40:   Sure?

ISH62:   Only speak when I am sure.

ISH34:   Found a pencil! Half used! Imagine real millennial hands using this?

ISH84:   More books.

ISH34:   Do not need any more books. Have enough.

ISH84:   Do we need any of this?

ISH62:   Yes, some objects. Contributes to the realism of the museum.

                  ISH34 holds up headphones.

ISH34:	To warm ears?
ISH40:	No, to listen to music. Called *headphones*.
ISH62:	Keep!

ISH62 takes the headphones and puts them on the table of props for the museum.

ISH40:	Smaller ones were called ear buds.
ISH20:	You know so much.
ISH62:	Ish is a music expert.
ISH20:	I adore music.
ISH40:	Millennial music?
ISH20:	Any kind of music.

ISH40 goes looking for ear buds.

ISH40:	We should listen to some of their music as an exercise!
ISH20:	Yes!
ISH62:	Would rather we did not.
ISH40:	Why not?
ISH62:	Always the same thing over and over again: "I love you, I need you, let's do it, let's do it, let's do it."
ISH40:	Part of the historical record.
ISH62:	Find the old horny lyrics tiresome.
ISH84:	Poor ancestors could not control themselves.
ISH40:	They could, but they did not.
ISH62:	In need of some serious hormonal rebalancing.

ISH20:   Do you think that is what saved us?

ISH84:   Think it was externalized reproduction that saved us. Freed women from the burdens of—

ISH62:   Now is not the time to discuss our salvation. Focus on the present task. Continue sorting.

ISH34:   *(Placing objects on the table.)* Pens, pins, pens, more paper, paper clips.

ISH20:   String—so much string.

ISH34:   Not string, wires.

                    ISH34 starts collecting old mobile phones from the pile.

ISH84:   Is it safe to touch those?

ISH40:   Too old to be dangerous, the bad part removed long, long ago.

ISH34:   Shells of their former selves.

                    ISH34 keeps collecting phones—how many more can there be?

                    ISH84 holds up a slim, deteriorating square.

ISH84:   A photograph.

                    ISH20 finds an old tube of lipstick, marvels at it quietly.

ISH40:   The last days of printed photography. A good find.

ISH84:   Beautiful.

                    ISH62 looks at the photograph, shrugs.

                    ISH20 has a look at the photograph.

ISH20:   Photograph of a woman and her child!

ISH62:   We do not know that it is the woman's child.

ISH84:   Seems likely though.

ISH62:   No room for what is likely. Must remain in the
              realm of facts, not conjecture.

              *ISH84 puts down the photograph, picks up
              a piece of newspaper.*

ISH84:   What about a newspaper?

ISH62:   Yes. Keep. The last days of newspaper, too.

ISH34:   Look how many phones! Who wants one?

              *ISH34 starts handing out the mobile
              phones—two or three per person—except
              to ISH62 who disapproves of this joke. They
              all start pretending to talk or type on their
              phones, alternating between their many
              phones.*

ISH62:   Funny. Very funny. But no. Not yet. Should
              not exaggerate.

ISH34:   Is it an exaggeration?

ISH62:   Yes. One phone each at the most. It is only
              1999 in our house. No explosion with phones
              quite yet.

              *ISH62 collects the phones, places two on the
              table and tosses the others aside.*

              *ISH34 holds up something vaguely
              electronic that is unrecognizable.*

ISH34:   What?

ISH40:   Could be...

ISH62:   Anything.

ISH20:   Looks sad.

                A reverent pause while they all consider
                this curious object of technology.

ISH84:   All of it looks somewhat sad... *(ISH84 steps*
                away from the mound of objects, slouches on a
                chair.) I feel unwell.

ISH62:   Must be the dusting. Think we have had
                enough with this. I will clean up. All of you
                should go to the topiaries for some breathing.

                ISH34 escorts ISH84 out, followed by
                ISH20.

                ISH40 is about to leave with them, but
                ISH62 calls out—

ISH62:   Before you go!

ISH40:   Yes?

ISH62:   Wanted to, uh... Are you mentoring the
                young one?

ISH40:   Am happy to feed the curiosity of all the
                volunteers—

ISH62:   Ish laughs a lot.

ISH40:   A good sense of humour.

ISH62:   Around you.

ISH40:   Only because I joke.

ISH62:   Ish always volunteers for anything you lead,
                never with me.

ISH40:   Because you do not joke.

ISH62:   Do not think that is all.

ISH40:   Also interested in my tasks.

            Momentary pause.

ISH62:   Interested in being a girl.

ISH40:   Is this about that?

ISH62:   Are you interested in bringing back anything from the past?

ISH40:   Am a historian, am merely curious about the past.

ISH62:   Careful. Would not want the work we are doing here to be mistaken as revivalist.

ISH40:   Would never let that happen. You know that. Besides, ish does not *really* want to be a—

            ISH20 appears at the door, looks to ISH40 with a flirtatious smile.

ISH20:   Are you coming?

ISH40:   Yes, coming!

ISH20:   Was worried we lost you to more work—like a real millennial dad!

ISH40:   Ha! Never. Will be with you in a moment.

ISH20:   Sure. Will wait outside.

            ISH20 twirls out the door as ISH40 turns to face a stern ISH62.

ISH62:   Like I said: careful.

            ISH40 nods and then walks nonchalantly out the door.

Scene 7

> *Late evening, a small light on ISH84 seated at a table where ish sews the Jennifer Aniston dress by hand. ISH62 enters, watches ISH84 work.*

ISH62:   Could have made it with a machine.

ISH84:   Authentic process. Almost done.

> *ISH84 turns the fabric about, makes some final touches.*

ISH62:   They rarely made their own dresses at that time. Most people would have gone to the mall to buy their—

ISH84:   This is no mall dress! This is *couture*.

ISH62:   Right. Am still not sure couture belongs in a millennial suburban house.

ISH84:   It belongs if we let it belong.

ISH62:   Anything belongs if we let it belong—does not make it the right thing to do.

ISH84:   Let us let this belong. Promise it will be a draw!

ISH62:   Am sure.

> *ISH84 finishes making the dress and then holds it up to show off the final product.*

ISH84:   See!

ISH62:   *(Feeling the dress.)* Impressive. Definitely does not belong to the everyday.

ISH84:   Is that a compliment?

ISH62:   A compliment to your craftwork.

ISH84:   Thank you.

ISH62:   Think we have done enough for today.

ISH84:   Yes. Let us go.

                *ISH62 and ISH84 get up, turn off the lights
                and exit, leaving the dress behind on the
                table.*

                *ISH20 walks into the shadowed house,
                tiptoes over to the box with the shoes, takes
                them out, and puts them on again. ISH20
                then walks around trying to be elegant in
                the heels but looking rather clumsy.*

                A sound startles ISH20.

ISH20:   Hello? Who is there?

                ISH40 appears at the door.

ISH40:   You came back for the shoes.

ISH20:   So sorry.

ISH40:   Do not be sorry. Hoped you might come back
                for them.

ISH20:   You did?

                ISH40 approaches ISH20.

ISH40:   Yes. Followed you here, actually. You look…

ISH20:   Say it.

ISH40:   Lovely.

ISH20:   Thank you.

ISH40:   Have something else to show you.

                ISH40 produces a box.

ISH20:   Not another pair!

ISH40:   Yes, but—well, for me.

                ISH40 opens the box, shows the contents.

ISH20:   Millennial businessman shoes!?

ISH40:   Yes!

ISH20:   Also real?

ISH40:   Also real.

ISH20:   Put them on!

                ISH40 sits down, puts on the shoes, then stands up and walks around in a small circle to show them off.

ISH20:   You look—dapper.

ISH40:   A good word that is. *Dapper.*

ISH20:   Not just any word, but a word that should belong to you. What do we do now?

ISH40:   Walk around.

                ISH40 and ISH20 walk around in their millennial shoes as though they might be people walking around a city, and when they cross one another's paths ISH40 nods and ISH20 gives a demure curtsy.

ISH20:   What else should we do in our shoes?

ISH40:   Could dance.

ISH20:   Have music?

ISH40:   Have to pretend!

                ISH20 pretends. Imaginary music starts to play—and maybe the audience can hear it too.

ISH20:	Oh, I can hear it! Only do not know how they danced.
ISH40:	Well. Uh. They—they danced like...

ISH40 starts to dance awkwardly on the spot.

ISH20 tries to replicate the moves, though with greater femininity.

ISH20:	Like this?
ISH40:	Yes! Or something like that. You are a fantastic dancer!
ISH20:	Have never tried before.
ISH40:	Not true!
ISH20:	True!

ISH40 takes ISH20's hand, and they dance together—though at a safe distance.

ISH40:	Do you like this?
ISH20:	Yes.
ISH40:	Good. Me too.

Their dancing is somewhat romantic. ISH40 suddenly pulls ISH20 in—almost too abruptly—and their dancing stops. Perhaps the music disappears. Are they about to kiss? ISH20 jumps back and almost falls over in the heels.

ISH40:	Are you all right?

ISH20 takes another step back.

ISH20:	This is not appropriate.
ISH40:	We are only dancing.

ISH20:   Could lead to more.

ISH40:   More what?

                ISH20 takes yet another step back.

ISH20:   Something like what they used to do.

ISH40:   What?

ISH20:   You know!

ISH40:   Say the word.

ISH20:   No. Must remain within the confines of the project at hand.

ISH40:   Is that what you want?

ISH20:   Yes. *(Quick pause.)* No. *(Quicker pause.)* Do not know. Yes. Yes, it is. Careful!

ISH40:   Then I will go.

                ISH40 bows, turns to leave.

ISH20:   Wait! Your heels!

ISH40:   *Your* heels. All yours.

                ISH40 exits. ISH20 is alone in the house, looks around as though lost for a moment before noticing the dress.

                ISH20 picks up the dress, strokes the fabric, and then holds it up alongside the shoes. Perfect together!

                ISH20 tucks the dress underarm and walks out of the house.

Scene 8

Move-in day!

ISH84 wanders the house, looking in the cupboards, under furniture, etc.

ISH62 carries a lamp into the room and tries it in several places.

ISH34 and ISH40 carry a variety of large items into the house (perhaps a sideboard, a sofa, chairs, etc.).

ISH20 carries a box into the kitchen, starts unpacking its contents (perhaps cookbooks, a blender, a stand with hanging mugs, etc.).

ISH84:   Cannot find it. Did you take the dress away?

ISH62:   Why would I do that?

ISH84:   You did not like the idea of the dress.

ISH62:   If I did not want it here, would have told you. Did you look upstairs?

ISH84:   We never put anything upstairs.

ISH62:   All of the costumes are upstairs.

ISH84 goes upstairs.

ISH62:   Is that all the major items?

ISH34:   Few more things.

ISH62:   Carry on. *(To ISH40.)* Need your help to position what is here.

ISH34 leaves and, over next few lines, returns with one or two things at a time — perhaps dining chairs, cushions, etc.

ISH40:   Start with?

ISH62:   Sofa.

ISH40:   Huge.

ISH62:   Heart of the living room. Heart of their house. Let us line it up to face out.

> *They drag the sofa to the centre of the living room — maybe it is starting to look like the living room in a 90's sitcom.*

ISH40:   Take our time! Priceless artifact. Few of this era's sofas still left.

ISH62:   So big.

ISH40:   Not so big for this house.

ISH62:   Millennials were all about comfort.

ISH40:   You take issue with comfort?

ISH62:   Implies laziness.

ISH40:   Implies hard work, need for bodily restoration.

> *ISH34 stops, looks at placement of furniture with puzzled look.*

ISH34:   Very ugly.

ISH40:   You have to see it as they saw it. Where is the TV? Need to get the TV.

> *ISH34 spins around, retrieves the TV hiding behind something.*

ISH62:   In front of the sofa.

> *ISH34 positions the TV in front of the sofa.*

ISH40:   We are making a universe here. This is their sun! *(ISH40 sits on the sofa facing the TV.)* After work, home. TV on. Dinner ready. I can see it all coming together.

ISH34 wanders off.

ISH62:   You have an idea of the past that I will never understand.

ISH40:   Just what is in the historical record.

ISH62:   Better go help find the dress.

ISH40:   What dress?

ISH62:   Ish made a dress. A movie-star dress. *(Sarcastically.)* A showstopper! If it can be found...

ISH62 goes up the stairs, and ISH20 comes out of the kitchen to sit next to ISH40 on the sofa.

ISH20:   Need to talk.

ISH40:   Am sorry about last night. If I was too—

ISH20:   You were not too—anything. Liked it. Made me feel what I think I always wanted to feel.

ISH40:   Can I see you again?

ISH20:   You are seeing me now.

ISH40:   Meant just the two of us. Alone. Promise to not try anything you do not want to do. You can trust me.

ISH20:   Do not trust myself.

ISH40:   I trust you.

ISH20:   Very nice of you to say, but—

ISH40:   Just to talk. And maybe try on our shoes together again. Walk around a little. That is all. No dancing, promise.

ISH20:   When?

ISH40:   Midnight.

                ISH84 follows ISH62 down the stairs, and ISH20 jumps up from the sofa.

ISH62:   Am sorry! Do not know where it could be.

ISH84:   Could not have just disappeared.

ISH62:   The potpourri bowl did!

ISH84:   The potpourri bowl was hideous.

ISH62:   And your dress is—what?

ISH84:   A lot of work!

ISH62:   Yes, I know. Work, work, work, work, work. Am so tired of hearing about your work. What do you think the rest of us are doing here?

ISH84:   If anyone sees a dress—

ISH62:   A very *pretty* dress, please let us know.

                ISH62 glances about the house, suddenly realizes that the recreated millennial house is almost complete.

ISH62:   Looks as though our work here is nearly done. Needs only a bit of tidying. Sure the dress will show up after that.

ISH40:   Can help you tidy. The rest of you go back to your personal spaces, get some alone time before our final practice tomorrow.

ISH84, ISH34, and ISH20 leave—ISH20 giving ISH40 a knowing look as ish exits.

Once alone, ISH62 and ISH40 survey the space.

ISH40:   Should get this all done before midnight, right?

ISH62:   Should hope so. *(A pause.)* When you are in the house—do you ever feel something?

ISH40:   Is this about me mentoring ish again?

ISH62:   So you are mentoring ish?

ISH40:   Not what I said.

ISH62:   Fine. You tell me there is no reason to be concerned, I trust you. What I mean to say is, whenever I am alone in the house— sometimes I feel—something.

ISH40:   Sad?

ISH62:   But sadness is such an old-fashioned idea— do you not think?

ISH40:   Do feelings go out of fashion?

ISH62:   In any event, it is more than a feeling. Like a presence, like someone is watching me. Or maybe it is just nervousness.

ISH40:   About?

ISH62:   So close to getting it right and just as close to getting it all wrong.

ISH40:   You think?

ISH62:   Closer to getting it wrong if we do not get back to work!

ISH40:	Right. Work: the great cure-all.
ISH62:	Spoken like a true millennial.
ISH40:	Feels like I could be. A real millennial, that is.
ISH62:	What a terrible idea!

> *They share a brief, synchronized laugh, and then start to tidy frantically.*

Scene 9

> *The empty and dark house at midnight.*
>
> *ISH40 enters quietly, cautiously.*

ISH40:	Hello? Is anybody—hello? *(Pause.)* I am here, are you here?
ISH20:	*(From upstairs.)* Are you alone?
ISH40:	Yes. Come down? I can turn on the lights.
ISH20:	No! I want you to see me in the moonlight.
ISH40:	There is no moonlight all the way down here.
ISH20:	Pretend!

> *Suddenly it is almost as if there is moonlight in the room.*
>
> *ISH20 descends the staircase wearing the Jennifer Aniston dress, heels, and maybe even a woman's wig like the hairstyle Aniston popularized in the 1990s.*
>
> *ISH20 no longer looks like an ish but a she—if with somewhat exaggerated feminine features.*

ISH40:   Was not expecting this.

ISH20:   Decided to do something special for you.

ISH40:   Pretty.

ISH20:   You think?

ISH40:   No, more than pretty. You are...stunning.

ISH20:   Stop!

ISH40:   We are becoming so old style!

ISH20:   What do we do now?

> *ISH40 takes ISH20 by the hand and they go to the sofa to sit.*

ISH40:   Comfortable, yes?

ISH20:   Is a bit tight, actually.

ISH40:   But the cushions are so fulsome!

ISH20:   Thought you meant the dress.

ISH40:   The dress is not comfortable?

ISH20:   No, but does not matter. Part of the historical record. Will adapt.

ISH40:   Right.

> *An awkward pause.*

ISH20:   What do we do now?

ISH40:   Pretend we are watching TV?

ISH20:   Good idea!

> *They stare straight ahead for a bit, seem bored.*

ISH40:   Not a very good program.

ISH20:   No.

ISH40:   Want me to change the channel?

ISH20:   Please.

                      ISH40 mimes changing the channel.

ISH40:   This?

ISH20:   If you like this.

ISH40:   Want something we both like.

ISH20:   Was there anything both a husband and wife enjoyed on TV?

ISH40:   Supposed to be father and daughter, remember?

ISH20:   Oh. Yes. Right. Forgot! For a moment thought of myself as the woman of the house. Must be the dress.

ISH40:   Suppose we could pretend to be that too. Just for tonight. Let us turn this off.

                      ISH40 mimes turning off the TV.

                      Awkward silence.

ISH20:   What else did millennial husbands and wives do on the sofa?

                      ISH40 turns to face ISH20, takes in a big whiff.

ISH40:   You smell nice.

ISH20:   Did they smell one another like that?

ISH40:   Sometimes. If they wore perfumes. You smell like—lilacs—peonies—wild roses. A garden.

ISH20:   And you smell like... *(ISH20 leans forward, smells ISH40.)* A forest.

ISH40:   A garden and a forest go together nicely, I think.

                Awkward laughter.

ISH20:   Now what?

                They are so close that what happens next seems inevitable.

ISH40:   Now, maybe we do—this?

                They kiss. Maybe it is robotic. Afterwards, ISH20 leans away.

ISH20:   Historically accurate?

ISH40:   Yes. But longer.

                A longer kiss.

ISH20:   Like that?

ISH40:   Even longer.

ISH20:   Until?

ISH40:   Until we want to take our clothes off.

ISH20:   Never want to take my clothes off with someone else.

ISH40:   Maybe because you have not kissed someone for long enough.

ISH20:   Do not think that will help.

ISH40:   What would help?

ISH20:   Tell me our story.

ISH40:   The story of you and me? Or the story of our characters?

ISH20:   You and me—as if we really were husband and wife.

ISH40:   Right. Our story, you and me, as husband and wife. Our story is—well, we met at the university where I teach.

ISH20:   Yes.

ISH40:   And—and—and I was your professor.

ISH20:   And?

ISH40:   And you were my student.

ISH20:   And how did we get from there to here?

ISH40:   Well, uh, from the moment I saw you I could not stop thinking of you.

ISH20:   Really?

ISH40:   Really. Could not stop thinking about— everything about you.

ISH20:   What about me?

ISH40:   Your voice. Your nose. Your laugh. Your walk. You have the most distinct walk. Did you know that? Could not stop thinking about all the things I wanted to tell you, to give you. Wanted to spend every minute of my life with you. Which is why I proposed to you, why I married you. So that I could buy this house with you and—and raise a family with you. Grow very old with you. So that we could be together until we die. Even want to die with you—at the very same minute, the very same second as you. Want everything with you— with you and only you.

ISH20:   Yes, understand now. Ready to take off my clothes with you.

ISH40:   Really?

ISH20:   Think so.

ISH40:   Me too.

ISH20:   Take me to the bedroom!

                ISH40 carries ISH20 up the stairs.

                End of Act One.

ACT TWO

Scene 1

The slow creep of a sunny morning.

ISH62 wanders around the house, making minor adjustments to the props, the furniture's placement, etc. Satisfied that everything is perfect, ISH62 goes to the base of the stairs and calls up.

ISH62: Ready?

ISH84: *(From upstairs.)* Ready!

ISH62: Then come down, take your places!

ISH34: *(From upstairs.)* Coming!

ISH62: Not *right* away. Will return in one minute. Remember: like you have never met me before, your first visitor to the millennial house!

> *ISH62 exits.*

> *ISH84, ISH40, ISH34, and ISH20 descend the staircase in their gendered millennial costumes—the men more masculine and the women more feminine than the typical middle-class millennial people they are trying to depict.*

ISH34, dressed as a sporty millennial teenage boy, stands by the entrance.

ISH40, dressed in a millennial man's suit, sits on the sofa and takes a remote control in hand as though changing the channels on the TV.

ISH20, dressed as a millennial teenage girl with an exaggerated amount of makeup, sits at the dining room table with a pen and pad of paper.

ISH84, dressed in a pastel sweater with jeans and a grey-haired wig, goes to the kitchen and starts assembling ingredients on the countertop.

ISH62 re-enters the house, awestruck.

ISH62:   Oooooooooooooooh—well—will-you-look-at—!

ISH34:   *(Stiffly.)* Heyyyyyyyy. Welcome to our millennial house.

ISH62:   Thank you.

ISH34:   What is up? *(Quickly:)* Built in 1999, this is the last freestanding millennial house in M City. Built when M City was a suburb. Before the Implosion and the subsequent Rebuild. Half a century before the Transition—

ISH62:   The *Great* Transition—

ISH34:   Before the *Great* Transition even began. It has survived all these years, up until now, for you. We are your...What is it again?

ISH62:   "We are your guides to the past."

ISH34:   Guides to the past!

ISH62:   Good. Slower, though. And with authenticity.

ISH34:   Meaning?

ISH62:   Normal voice.

ISH34:   Using my millennial voice.

ISH62:   Yes, I know. That is good. Only mean speak
            with ease. Now what?

            *An awkward pause while ISH62 waits for
            more from ISH34.*

ISH34:   Oh. I live here.

ISH62:   Remember ease.

ISH34:   Right. I *liiiiive* here. With my mom, dad, sister.

ISH62:   Indeed?

ISH34:   Yes. Mom is out, but the rest of us are here.

ISH62:   Remember it is fine to use words like *cool*,
            dude, and *badass*. And to add contractions.

ISH34:   Right. Cool. Dude. Badass. My *grandma's*
            visiting for the month. She drives my dad
            craaaaaaazy.

ISH84:   Should ish really be the first one to greet
            visitors?

ISH62:   Is fine.

ISH34:   Trying my best!

ISH62:   Is good. Now draw me in and through the
            museum.

ISH34:   Would you like to meet my dad?

ISH62:   I would. You do not have to ask. Just introduce
            me.

ISH34:	Right. He is just back from work.
ISH62:	What does he do for work?
ISH34:	Right. He's a registered professional accountant. Dad?
ISH40:	Yes, son?
ISH34:	We have a guest.

ISH34 guides ISH62 to meet the father and then starts wandering around the room, inspecting structural elements in the background.

ISH40:	Hello and welcome to our house. I'm the father of the household, and this is our living room. You'll notice that digitization has not yet entered our house. Instead, we like TVs. The bigger the better. Size is important, as men like me used to say.
ISH62:	A joke?
ISH40:	A sense of millennial humour.
ISH62:	Make sure that is clear. Do not want them to think we hold those same jokes.
ISH40:	Obviously.
ISH62:	Continue?
ISH40:	I get home from work every day at six. I take the commuter train home. It takes 47 minutes from downtown to this house—which was at quite a remove from the core when it was first built, before this became a core in its own right.
ISH62:	Visitor will not know what a core is.

ISH40:   An old city core. Millennial city core. Where
                financial—

ISH62:   But do not overwhelm them with informa-
                tion. Will bore them. Let visitors ask ques-
                tions—that is advice for all. Let the visitors
                discover!

ISH40:   Fine. Any questions?

ISH62:   No, because you have already told me
                everything.

ISH40:   Have not.

ISH62:   Making a point.

ISH40:   Point understood. Any questions?

ISH62:   What are you watching on the television?

ISH34:   Are we calling it "the television" or "the TV"?

ISH62:   Whichever. What are you watching?

ISH40:   I . . . do not know.

ISH62:   Men your age liked to watch sporting events,
                crime dramas, and the news.

ISH40:   Then I am watching the news.

ISH62:   What is happening in the news?

ISH40:   Conflicts.

ISH62:   Do we need to review the current millennial
                events again?

ISH84:   No. Please keep going. Ish is only teasing,
                pretending not to know.

ISH40:   Have you met my wife?

ISH62:   You mean daughter?

ISH40:   Yes, I meant daughter!

ISH62:   Your wife is out, remember? I will play your wife.

ISH40:   Right. Know that.

                ISH40 guides ISH62 to meet ISH20 at the dining room table.

                ISH20 looks up and the amount of makeup on ish face startles ISH62.

ISH62:   What is that?

ISH40:   My daughter!

ISH62:   I mean the face. Who did this to you?

ISH20:   My boyfriend likes my makeup.

ISH62:   Your boyfriend?

ISH20:   At high school.

ISH62:   Oh, you are in character.

ISH20:   I'm writing an essay about World War II. Boring! I'd rather be at the mall.

ISH62:   Do not forget to point out that you are writing by hand, that it would have been too expensive for everyone to have a personal computer in this household.

ISH20:   Yes and *(Removing a beeper from her belt.)* my boyfriend is paging me right now! He wants to meet at the mall.

ISH62:   Fine. Fine. This is fine. But you must take down that face.

ISH20:   Tilt it down?

ISH62:   The makeup, I meant.

ISH62 moves on to the kitchen.

ISH20:   I was not done.

ISH62:   Now what is going on in the kitchen?

ISH84:   Well, hello. I'm Grandma.

ISH62:   Try *Nana*. That is cozier.

ISH84:   I'm Nana. I'm baking!

ISH20:   What does ish mean by take down the makeup?

ISH62:   Too much paint on your face. I have moved on. Keep going.

ISH84:   I'm baking cookies.

ISH62:   Good use of contractions. Remember, baking was a novelty for them. Maybe for special occasions like Christmas.

ISH84:   Are we pretending it is Christmas?

ISH62:   No.

ISH20:   Think my face looks nice.

ISH40:   Is fine.

ISH20:   Just fine?

ISH40:   Lovely.

ISH84:   So what is the special occasion?

ISH62:   Nana is visiting! That is special occasion enough!

ISH84:   Oh. Right. Many people would have used baking mixes from a grocery store, but I'm *baking-from-scratch*!

ISH62:	What are you baking?
ISH84:	Chocolate chippy cookies.
ISH62:	Just chip.

ISH20 bursts into the kitchen, followed by ISH40.

ISH20:	What is your problem with my face?
ISH62:	Not to discuss now, but is exaggerated.
ISH20:	I based it on a photograph from a celebrity magazine. Looked at the archives and everything!
ISH40:	Calm.
ISH62:	Let us continue with the cookies.
ISH20:	But this is *not* exaggerated.
ISH84:	I'm baking with my secret recipe.
ISH62:	A secret *family* recipe.
ISH20:	Why are you ignoring me?
ISH84:	Yes! A secret family—(*Suddenly noticing something in the living room.*) Ohhhhhhhhhh-hhhhhhhhhhhhh!
ISH62:	What?

ISH84 pulls the Jennifer Aniston dress—now torn—from some dark corner along the staircase.

ISH84:	My dress! My dress! My dress!

ISH84 holds up the dress, inspects the damage.

ISH62:	Suppose we cannot use it now.

ISH84:	Did you do this?
ISH62:	No!
ISH84:	But who?
ISH62:	Do not know. Back to the cookies.

ISH20 approaches, strokes the dress.

ISH20:	Is beautiful. Should be repaired. And then I could wear it in the house.
ISH84:	Oh, yes!
ISH62:	Absolutely not.
ISH84:	Why not?
ISH62:	Do not want to confuse the visitors! Your makeup is distraction enough.
ISH84:	But ish is the only one who would fit in my dress.
ISH62:	Not true. *(Turns to ISH34.)* Ish is also slender.
ISH34:	Am not sure.
ISH40:	Ish is our teenage son.
ISH62:	We could reassign the parts for the sake of the dress.
ISH40:	A bit late for that now.
ISH20:	*(Grasping for the dress.)* Oh, but I love it!
ISH62:	Our museum is not a place for love.
ISH84:	Is my dress and I want it to be worn by someone who will love it!

ISH62 sees something new in ISH84.

ISH62:	In that case, you love the dress.

ISH84:   Yes, of course I do.

ISH62:   You love the dress *and* you are talented
                enough to adjust the dress so that it could fit
                you.

ISH84:   Not sure that—

ISH62:   You must wear the dress!

                ISH62 takes the tattered dress and somehow
                drapes it over ISH84 so that ish is half-
                wearing the dress.

ISH84:   Was made for a different kind of—

ISH40:   Yes, ish is not the intended wearer for this
                kind of—

ISH62:   None of us are! It is a very old design.

ISH40:   Was meant to show off skin.

ISH84:   And my skin is—

ISH62:   Fantastic!

ISH84:   Just never thought of myself in something
                like this.

ISH62:   See! Now you sound like a real millennial
                woman! Always thinking of yourself last. I
                want *you* to put *you* first. No more worship
                of the young!

ISH20:   Why do you not like me?

ISH62:   My criticism is not personal.

ISH20:   Then what is the matter?

ISH62:   Historical accuracy.

ISH20:   But I am historically accurate.

ISH62:   No, you are not. You are a fabulist. You make the past look far prettier than it really was.

ISH20:   Fine.

                    ISH20 moves towards the stairs, about to go up.

ISH62:   Where are you going?

ISH20:   To make myself more historically accurate.

ISH62:   Taking down the makeup, then?

ISH20:   Yes. And maybe a few adjustments to my costume. Have something in mind that will be closer to what you want.

ISH62:   Good. Am glad.

ISH20:   Am glad you are glad. Will be as quick as I can. Promise.

                    ISH20 goes up the stairs.

ISH62:   Think ish finally understands what I have been trying to explain all along. Took some time, but we got there. Just needed a little patience—something millennials did not have. And that is another reason to be grateful to be living in the present: we have patience! *(To ISH84.)* Now, back into the kitchen, Nana.

ISH34:   Couture in the kitchen?

ISH84:   Yes, does not seem like the right place to wear a dress like this.

ISH62:   No place in this house would have been right for this dress. But you insisted on bringing it into our museum, so here we are with cookies and couture!

ISH34:   Maybe our grandma is extra fashionable.

ISH62:   Yes, maybe. And she is making her famous chocolate chip cookie recipe in her couture. Using her very special, secret ingredient— which is...

ISH84 goes back to the kitchen, starts to mix again.

ISH84:   Horseradish!

ISH62:   Horseradish?

ISH34:   What is that?

ISH40:   A spicy root.

ISH62:   Does not sound right.

ISH84:   You told me to come up with an interesting secret ingredient.

ISH62:   Was thinking something like rosewater.

ISH84:   Was very difficult to find horseradish. Had to go to the far end of the marketlands to get some.

ISH62:   All right. Horseradish it is.

ISH84:   Raw cookie dough was a millennial delicacy—

ISH62:   Not a delicacy, just a treat. We do not want to confuse our visitors too much.

ISH84:   Right. Will try again. Raw cookie dough was a very special millennial treat, something they sometimes ate without even baking the dough—when they were feeling sad or needed a pick-me-up. Who wants to try some?

ISH34:   I do! I do! I do!

ISH62:   Do not know if that is a good idea.

ISH34:   Thought we were going to serve samples to visitors.

ISH62:   That was the plan before the horseradish.

ISH34:   I want to try it anyway!

ISH62:   Maybe I should try it first. Just in case.

ISH84:   Have a taste off my wooden spoon!

ISH62 takes a mouthful of the cookie dough.

At the same time, ISH20 comes down the stairs dressed as a very pregnant woman — perhaps wearing a maternity dress, and a new, dowdier wig, looking much more haggard than before, almost as if to taunt ISH62 with this new depiction.

ISH20:   Hello, family! Your beloved mom is finally home!

ISH40:   *(Quietly, almost to ishself.)* Oh no.

ISH62 turns around and, on seeing ISH20, chokes out the cookie dough.

ISH34 and ISH84 seem delighted by this new character in the house.

ISH62:   What—are—you—doing?

ISH20:   You did not like it when I presented a pretty version of womanhood, so I have decided to present its ugly side instead.

ISH62:   But you are—you are—you are supposed to play our teenage daughter!

ISH20:   Was thinking I could play the mom instead.

ISH34:   Fun!

ISH84:   So excited to be a grandma—again!

ISH20:   Something I put together quickly, but think it works. *(ISH20 moves towards ISH40 for an opinion.)* What do you think?

ISH40:   Think that—

ISH62:   No!

ISH34 and ISH84: Yes! Yes! Yes!

ISH62:   *(To ISH34 and ISH84.)* No, no, no.

                ISH84 goes over to ISH20 and they walk to the sofa together.

ISH84:   Here, let Grandma help you get to the sofa!

ISH62:   This is not the story we agreed to tell!

ISH20:   The old story was not working—you made me realize that. Needed to adapt. Important to be flexible, roll with the punches. Something I understand as a mom. *(As if re-entering the performance of the museum's interpretation in this new character.)* Oh, we have guests! And I feel like a total slob. Please forgive me. I wasn't expecting anybody. Normally, I'd have my hair done, my makeup on, the house tidy and clean. Which is a lot for me to do because, in addition to being a mom, I work a full-time job as a dental hygienist!

ISH34:   Such a good role for you!

ISH84:   Yes, ish knows so much about millennial moms!

ISH20:   Unfortunately, as you can see, I'm about to have a baby—so I've let a lot of things slide around here. My back hurts, my belly aches, and my feet—you have no idea how swollen my feet are! *(To ISH40.)* Honey bear, could you come rub my feet?

ISH40 hesitates.

ISH40:   Should I still play the dad?

ISH20:   Of course, you should still play the dad. Now, get over here and rub my feet, hun!

ISH62:   *(Stands in front of ISH40.)* Do not move.

ISH20:   Husbands did this sort of thing. I read about it. I mean, it's the least he could do after he bred me so hard and so deep. Look at me! I'm a whale!

ISH62:   This language is—revolting!

ISH20:   Am only playing a part.

ISH62:   No suburban mother would have used language like that.

ISH20:   How do you know? *(To ISH40.)* Honey bear— my feet?

ISH62:   (To ISH40.) Stop ish!

ISH20:   Stop calling me ish. I am her now.

ISH40 takes a cautious step towards ISH20.

ISH40:   Do you not think it might be a little late in the project to include the role of a pregnant mother?

ISH20:   Oh, c'mon, folks! We're doing fine here. My feet?

ISH84:   Such wonderful millennial parlance, too!

ISH62:   Cannot believe this is happening.

ISH34:   Maybe we should all rub mom's feet.

ISH84:   Great idea!

           ISH34 and ISH84 rush over to ISH20s feet
           and begin to massage them.

ISH62:   Stop!

ISH34:   Ohhhhhhhh, yes! Feels so good! Honey bear, you could learn a thing from Grandma and your son.

ISH62:   Stop, stop, stop. All of you must stop!

ISH34:   Why?

ISH84:   Yes, think this a much more interesting portrayal of motherhood than yours.

ISH62:   My portrayal was not a silly exaggeration that glorified the pregnancy experience!

ISH20:   Am not glorifying anything. Look at my feet!

ISH62:   You are making a mockery of this project, my project, my lifelong dream! All of you. *(Pries ISH34 and ISH84 off of ISH20 and pushes them away, then addresses ISH20 directly.)* But you most of all. You, who should not even be here. Because this is a museum to help people—people like you—whose ignorance about the past threatens to bring it all back. Have had enough!

           ISH62 reaches under ISH20's dress for the object — maybe some sort of pillow — that creates the pregnancy shape.

           A brief struggle.

> *ISH62 eventually triumphs and pulls away the pregnancy object.*

ISH62:   Aha!

ISH20:   My baby!

ISH62:   Is not a baby! Is no more than a—

ISH20:   Somebody please help me get my baby back!

ISH34:   Do not know what to do.

ISH20:   *(Almost in tears.)* Was going to call it Maddison if it was a girl, Cody if it was a boy—

ISH84:   Oh, beautiful names for a millennial baby!

ISH62:   Stop this silly performance.

ISH20:   Please do not hurt my—

ISH62:   THIS IS NOT A BABY!

> *ISH62 does something to destroy the pregnancy object, to take it apart, and then scatters its insides—maybe feathers or cotton fluff—around the room, making a mess.*

See! Not—a—baby!

> *A tense pause. ISH20 takes a deep breath or two, and then—*

ISH20:   I understand.

ISH62:   You do?

ISH20:   You are jealous.

ISH62:   Of what?

ISH20:   Of how well I understand the past.

ISH62:   Ha!

ISH20:   And I understand it so well because I have experienced more of it than you ever will.

ISH62:   What are you talking about?

ISH20:   I have experienced breeding.

           A confused pause.

ISH62:   Are you playing the mother part right now or are you being—yourself?

ISH20:   Myself. And as myself, I have experienced breeding. *(Takes ISH40's hand.)* We both have.

ISH40:   Uh, well, we, uh—

           ISH40 pulls away from ISH20's handhold.

ISH62:   *(To ISH40.)* What is ish saying?

IHS40:   Well, I—

ISH62:   *(Still on ISH40.)* You let this happen. Told me you were not doing this. Told me you were not doing anything more than work on the project. And I believed you. All the while you were off breeding!

ISH34:   Do not understand. Thought breeding was impossible for us.

ISH62:   Yes, of course, breeding is impossible for us.

ISH40:   We only tried something *like* breeding.

ISH20:   Was close enough to the real thing for me.

ISH62:   *(To ISH40.)* How could you do this to me? How could you let this happen to my museum!

ISH84:   Thought it was *our* museum.

ISH40:   Calm. Let me explain before you—

ISH62:   What is there to explain?

ISH40:   Was only research.

ISH62 and ISH20: Research?

ISH40:   Was always curious about bedroom history, but knew that that did not interest you, so undertook the project on my own. Did not think it would get in the way of the museum. Thought of it as side research, if you will.

ISH20:   Was more than side research.

ISH40:   No, was not.

ISH20:   But it was—what we had—we had...love.

ISH62:   Love?

ISH40:   Maybe they told one another that that was love—a long, long time ago. But from our little experiment, have drawn the conclusion that it was no more than a charade people performed to cope with the stark realities of their lives.

ISH62:   Such as?

ISH40:   Such as the reality that houses like this were no more than sites for both resting and breeding.

ISH20:   Sites?

ISH62:   Is that some sort of conclusion?

ISH40:   Have to reflect on this some more, review my notes—but this is how I am thinking about it for now.

ISH20:	Then...you do not love me?
ISH40:	No.

ISH20 realizes the truth of the project— maybe removes the wig, the costume.

ISH20:	Am a fool.
ISH40:	Would not say that.
ISH62:	I would—both of you have been fools.
ISH20:	Yes. Have to go. Am sorry I ever came here.

ISH20 exits quickly from the house.

All seem unsure what to do next, and then—

ISH62:   Is fine, is fine. Everything is fine. Can move ahead with the project without ish. I can still play the mother, was going to do that all along. And do not need the teenage daughter—irrelevant part. I will go get my mother costume, and then we can carry on with the rehearsal.

ISH84:   No. No more.

ISH62:   But we open the museum tomorrow. Must keep practising.

ISH84 takes off the dress, the wig.

ISH84:   Have had enough of this.

ISH62:   Do not give up now! Have to help people remember the past—especially the next generation, which, as you have witnessed today, is starting to forget!

ISH84:   But none of us *really* remembers. Am the oldest one here—knew people who were alive when this house was built!—and still never got it right. Dress was too pretty. Secret ingredient was wrong. Called myself Grandma when I should have used Nana. The mistakes are paralyzing. At best, the past is a guessing game, and I am tired of guessing.

ISH62:   Perhaps you just need some alone time?

ISH34:   *(Maybe removing a part of the millennial costume.)* Am also tired of guessing.

ISH62:   But you have put so much work into the structure.

ISH34:   Am happy to know the structure is now secure—that is enough for me.

ISH84:   No small feat.

ISH62:   But what is the point of securing the structure if nobody gets to see its inside?

ISH34:   Maybe we could still let people see the inside—without us. A museum without our characters. Just the inside. Would only need to put away the costumes, tidy things, affix the furniture and props in place.

ISH84:   Maybe display the dress somewhere?

ISH34:   Could do that, too. Enough time before tomorrow, so that the museum could still open on anniversary day.

ISH40:   Not a terrible idea.

ISH34:   People would still learn about the past—but without any of us getting in the way.

ISH62:   A good point.

ISH34:   You like the idea?

ISH62:   Like the idea. Characters were not working anyway. All of us could see that. What matters is the space. Would be interesting for people to simply see where they lived.

ISH84:   So—what now?

                Maybe ISH62 starts to scurry around, almost manically—as if trying to fix the project but not sure where to begin first.

ISH62:   Like you said: tidy, costumes away, affix the furniture in place. Work to do!

                ISH34 and ISH84 exit with a new sense of purpose.

                ISH62 is about to start work on something, but ISH40 stands in the way.

ISH40:   Am sorry.

ISH62:   Do not believe you.

ISH40:   Did not realize what I was doing.

ISH62:   Of course, you did—knew the young one had fantastical ideas about the past.

ISH40:   Just thought it would be an interesting starting point.

ISH62:   We do not need starting points anymore. Humanity, I mean. We had our struggle, and now here we are: at this most peaceful point in time. There is no need to go back on this. *(ISH40 shrugs, unsure.)* Do not think we can work together anymore.

The idea is saddening to both of them.

ISH40:   Have worked together for a long time.

ISH62:   A long time. But think you need something new, now.

ISH40:   Maybe.

ISH62:   So go ahead, do something new. But be careful: nothing old is ever new.

ISH40:   Know that now.

ISH62:   But before you go, think we should see this museum through together.

ISH40:   Agreed.

ISH62:   So—work to do?

ISH40:   Yes. Work to do.

ISH40 watches ISH62 march off purposefully to do more work and then meanders in a different direction.

Scene 2

Now out of their millennial costumes, ISH34 and ISH84 tidy the house, secure the furniture, etc. Perhaps ISH84 hangs the dress up in a closet. They stop, look around.

ISH34:   Looks much better.

ISH84:   (*Observing slowly.*) Mmmmm. Think I am a lot like this house.

ISH34:   You are not at all like this house!

ISH84:   House is very old. Still standing, but needs help. Everything fixed in place, now, unmoving. Quiet, too. Nearly forgotten.

ISH34:   Until tomorrow!

ISH84:   Yes, hope someone comes to discover the house tomorrow.

ISH34:   Expect crowds!

ISH84:   Will see.

ISH34:   Sad you do not get to play grandma?

ISH84:   No. Think I am probably something like a grandma, anyway. Do not need the hair, or the clothes, or those terrible cookies. Besides, was not the real reason I did this.

ISH34:   What was the real reason?

ISH84:   Boredom. I think.

ISH34:   Think I was bored before, too.

ISH84:   What will you do now?

ISH34:   Do not know.

ISH84:   No more engineering projects?

ISH34:   No. A waste.

ISH84:   Nothing is ever a waste.

ISH34:   It is! Spent all my life worrying about the collapse of buildings only to find out we ishes are the delicate ones.

ISH84:   Delicate but resilient. We always find a way to continue.

ISH34:   And how will you continue—now that our work here is done.

ISH84:   Do not know yet. Becomes more difficult at my age. You are lucky: there is still time for you to try just about anything.

ISH34:   Still time for you to try a lot of things, too.

ISH84:   Some things, yes.

ISH34:   Think I want to be your friend.

ISH84:   As in—the same way those other two wanted to be friends?

ISH34:   No! Nothing like that. I do not have that kind of desire.

ISH84:   What kind of desire, then?

ISH34:   The desire for time with another human being. Time without purpose. And often! At least twice a week. But never scheduled.

ISH84:   Sounds vestigial.

ISH34:   Might be old-fashioned, but that is what I want.

ISH84:   Maybe it is what I want, too. What I have wanted all along. But maybe it is impossible. Utopias do not exist.

ISH34:   Not asking for a utopia, just friendship.

ISH84:   We could try.

ISH34:   When can we start?

ISH84:   Maybe we already have.

ISH34:   Right.

ISH84:   So, what should we—as friends—do now?

ISH34:   Perhaps a walk?

ISH84:   To where?

ISH34:   Any place, really.

ISH84:   For what?

ISH34:   It cannot have a purpose, remember? This will be difficult at first, but we should try purposelessness.

ISH84:   I am willing to try. Really I am.

ISH34:   Good. I am glad. So am I.

ISH84:   Shall we?

              They lock arms and walk very slowly out of the house.

Scene 3

A dull sunlight on the empty house, several days later.

ISH40 looks about, alone.

ISH20 walks into the house cautiously.

They are surprised to see one another.

ISH40:   You came back.

ISH20:   Did not expect to find anybody here.

ISH40:   Thought we would abandon the project?

ISH20:   Maybe.

ISH40:   Opened it as a museum without the charac-
          ters. Just a space for people to discover on
          their own.

ISH20:   And what have people been discovering so
          far?

ISH40:   No visitors yet.

ISH20:   Oh.

ISH40:   Has only been a couple of days.

ISH20:   Right. *(A shift.)* Was what we did…?

ISH40:   Yes?

ISH20:   Was it really only research?

ISH40:   Yes. *(Quick pause.)* No. *(Quick pause.)* Do not
          know. Started as research.

ISH20:   And then?

ISH40:   And then—stopped recording my findings.

ISH20:   Why?

ISH40:   Did not want them to be just findings.

ISH20:   Right.

ISH40:   Am sorry. For leading you—unknowingly—
          into my little experiment.

ISH20:   Led myself into it, I think.

ISH40:   Let us say that we led one another into it?

ISH20:   Maybe.

ISH40:   What brought you back to the museum?

ISH20:   Is silly.

ISH40:   Tell me anyway?

ISH20:	Was hoping I might come back and find ghosts.
ISH40:	Ghosts?
ISH20:	Of the people who used to live here.
ISH40:	Why would you want to see their ghosts?
ISH20:	To ask them if we got it right. Our museum. The way we tried to be them. But also the way we live now.
ISH40:	And what do you think they would tell you?

A reflective pause followed by laughter.

ISH20:	I have no idea! And that was why I hoped to find them here.
ISH40:	But you found me instead. Disappointed?
ISH20:	No. Never.

They exchange a look of compassion for one another.

ISH40:	Oh! Have something for you!

ISH40 turns around and retrieves a small bundle from somewhere in the museum. ISH20 opens it to discover the teenage girl costume—perhaps with the wig and the heels.

ISH20:	Do not think I want this anymore. Thought it was what I wanted, but…was not. The breeding, also not what I wanted. Not that you were bad at—whatever that was. As historically accurate as you could have been.
ISH40:	Thank you.
ISH20:	Just—not what I was looking for.

ISH40:	And what are you looking for?
ISH20:	Still trying to figure that out.
ISH40:	Me too.
ISH20:	Maybe the ghosts could help us with that.
ISH40:	Think I am done dwelling down here in the past. For now, at least.
ISH20:	Maybe see you again sometime—outside of the museum.
ISH40:	Yes. Back in the land of the living.

ISH40 exits.

Alone, ISH20 looks down at the costume in hand as though it might have belonged to a departed loved one. ISH20 smells the clothes and then lays them on the floor in the shape of a body, a woman—the ghost ISH20 was most hoping to find.

ISH20 kneels to kiss the clothes on the floor—the way one might kiss the body of a loved one goodbye at a wake.

A moment later, ISH20 stands up and slowly backs away from the shape of the clothes, ready to return to the land of the living and begin anew.

End of play.